Praise for *The Courage Coach*

"I could not put this book down! The Courage Coach is a badly needed resource not only for those seeking healing from abuse, but also for pastors, seminary students and Christian organizations and denominations committed to preventing and addressing abuse. It is not only a personal story but also practical! It demonstrates wisdom on every page, and is deeply rooted in a desire to serve others. Ashley says it best: 'Not only did you fail to destroy me, but now I will rescue others from your clutches.' It should be required reading for all seminary students. "

Mimi Haddad, President
Christians For Biblical Equality International

"The Courage Coach Book is clear, grace-embraced, and highly practical—for anyone living in the aftermath of abuse or those who want to help abuse survivors. Easter paints readers a clear picture of abuse and highlights the avenue toward genuine health."

Mary DeMuth, Author
Not Marked: Finding Hope and Healing after Sexual Abuse

"Ashley does a fantastic job of taking the incredibly complex issue of sexual abuse/assault and boiling it down to what every survivor needs to know; You are not alone, We are here for you, and here are some paths to help healing begin."

David Pittman, Executive Director
Together We Heal

"Ashley Easter is not just a fantastic writer and speaker but a significant, powerful voice - speaking up for the abused and broken. The Courage Coach helps readers easily understand abuse - the varying levels of severity as well as shining light on the abuse that happens inside the walls of the church and in Christian homes. Ashley writes with deep understanding that will make victims of abuse feel safe while also having an intensity that will help those who have not experienced abuse be more aware and empathetic to victims as well as know the signs to be looking for. Ashley gives victims of abuse the tools needed to identify what happened to them, find healing and hope, and ultimately find healing."

Sierra White, Founder
Ezer Rising

"Like any good coach, The Courage Coach not only instructs but affirms and encourages as well. The wealth of information never overwhelms and is gently expressed. I highly recommend it as an excellent resource for anyone who is struggling as a victim of abuse or for anyone who is helping a family member or friend who has experienced abuse."

Dianne Couts, President
MK Safety Net (Missionary Kid Safety Net)

The Courage Coach

THE COURAGE COACH

A Practical, Friendly Guide on How to Heal from Abuse

Ashley Easter

First paperback edition published in 2017. Raleigh, NC.

Designed by Jackson Dame of Bilateral Creative
    www.bilateralcreative.com

Edited by Elizabeth Hart

Cover photos: © AbdulRehman, © mikelaptev / Adobe Stock

The typefaces used are Adobe Caslon Pro for the body text and Semplicita Pro for the headers and chapter titles.

*"Courage, after all, is not the absence of fear.
It's the will to persevere even in the face of fear."*

- Christine Caine

Acknowledgments

I would like to extend a special thank you to
Boz Tchividjian, Dianne Couts,
Rachel Williams-Jordan, and David Pittman
for your gracious support in the creation of this book.

And to my husband, Will Easter.
You are my healer and my hero.
I love you forever and always.

Table of Contents

Foreword

I have been repeatedly struck by just how many abuse victims suffer in silence and isolation. I am a former abuse prosecutor, and for almost 20 years, I have served as the executive director of a non-profit that addresses abuse issues within faith communities. As a result of the cruelty victims experience, they often lose the ability or the strength to reach out and shout out.

When some victims finally take a courageous yet trembling step forward out of the shadows, their religious communities often chastise or disbelieve them, aggravating their suffering. Oftentimes, religious communities respond to abuse disclosures with distorted spiritual directives that push the wounded back into the shadows, convinced that is what God wants.

Victims often find themselves greatly confused and with so many unanswered questions. Is this even abuse? Is it my fault? Is this God's will for my life? Tragically, because of the isolation forced upon them, many abuse victims have nowhere to turn for informed answers – which are often the first steps toward freedom and healing. As a result, they remain silent and isolated, stuck in the shadows of a dark and painful world, eventually giving up hope.

There is hope.

I met Ashley Easter a few years ago after she took the courageous step forward to come to terms with her own past abuse. Ashley has a passionate commitment to help and empower victims who are stuck in a world of abuse, isolation, and silence. Based upon her own life experience, she understands the difficulty of stepping out from the shadows and the many risks involved.

If you know Ashley, you know how she has channeled her commitment and passion into action. She lives out her advocacy in more ways than I can describe in a foreword. Ashley spends her days (and nights) walking alongside countless abuse victims who are struggling to step forward, and last year, she organized The Courage Conference. More conferences are already planned, and they focus on providing abuse victims with a safe space to hear from others who have walked similar journeys and who understand the many complex dynamics associated with different types of abuse. One thing I love most about The Courage Conference is that victims who are isolated and are unable to attend in person can access it online. Ashley supports to the wounded where they are, helps to answer their questions, and empowers them to step forward into the arms of those who will welcome, affirm, and serve them.

The Courage Coach is yet another powerful and very practical way that Ashley has turned her commitment into action. This amazing book must get into the hands of those suffering from abuse. In simple but profound ways, this resource is the friend that so many abuse victims need but do not have. Through her writing, Ashley befriends readers, answers the tough questions, and addresses so many of the issues that keep victims stuck in the toxic and destructive cycle of abuse. From the perspective of a close friend, Ashley will help readers answer questions such as, Is This Abuse? Why Was I Abused? What Should I Do Now? What Are My Rights? What Should I Expect From Others? How Can I Move Forward Towards Healing? If you are an abuse victim, I believe that the answers to these questions in the forthcoming pages can and will be your first steps on a courageous journey of freedom, healing, and hope. If you are not an abuse victim, let these pages provide you with the tools necessary to serve the wounded who may reach out and possibly step out from the shadows of abuse.

I am grateful for Ashley Easter as she lives out the beautiful truth that the suffering people of this world are not alone and have a value that no one can take away from them. May we all learn to love in this way.

Boz Tchividjian
Executive Director, GRACE
www.netgrace.org

DEAR READER,

I want you to know that picking up this book and opening its pages is an act of courage. How do I know? Because I remember the feeling I had the first time I read a book on abuse. I had experienced some pretty hurtful things, and I had a lot of questions.

On one hand, I wanted to find answers to the burning questions inside of me. Questions such as: This hurts, but is it abuse? Is it my fault that I have been treated this way? Has anyone else ever felt this way before? Is there anything I can do to feel happy again? On the other hand, I was afraid to find out the answers. It seemed easier just to maintain the status quo, apologize again for something I hadn't done, and keep my head down.

Have you asked yourself any of these questions? Can you identify with these feelings? If so, I want you to know that you are not alone. I get it. While I can't know exactly how you are feeling, I know what it is like to experience treatment that did not feel safe or good. I have lived through abuse, and felt that wave of anxiety wash over me as I looked toward freedom. I needed a North Star to guide me toward truth, freedom, and light.

You see, I experienced multiple instances of abuse by multiple perpetrators. And every time I began to have an inkling that what was happening was wrong, I felt like I was on a threshold. Do I stay here and hope things get better or do I follow the North Star and find out the answers to my questions? Maybe, just maybe, I will find happiness and freedom. Ultimately, I chose freedom, and my life has been so much better for it.

As I followed my North Star, I wished that some-one who understood could have coached me along the way. I needed someone who had been there and could encourage me from a place of experience. For me, the scariest part of finding happiness and freedom was not knowing who to trust for answers and trying to figure out what I should or could do next. I had no idea how people would respond to me when I began to share the realization of abuse, and I had to fumble around and figure out what to do on my own. I longed for a trustworthy friend to guide me to safety.

I decided to write this book as a guide for others as they seek safety, and as a friend who had gone before to lead the way. I pray this book answers some of your tough questions and illuminates the different pathways to healing so you can choose your best route. My hope for this book is that it is a source of comfort and healing for you. I hope by the end, we will be trusted friends.

After experiencing abuse, I eventually found the help and support I needed to get free of the abuse, to begin healing, and to enjoy my life. I had no idea what was possible for my life. The more healing I gain, the more happiness I can let in. I still have dark days, but those are occurring less often. And without those shackles of abuse holding me back, I am beginning to live to my full potential. I am creating a life motivated by love rather than fear or shame. I am choosing relationships that are healthy and empowering rather than oppressive and controlling. I am doing the things I have always wanted to do and am at a place where I can reach out and join hands with others.

I connected with a group of experts and studied with a local domestic violence prevention center. I became a certified abuse victim advocate. I now spend most of my time supporting others who experienced abuse similar to my own. I write articles and speak on how abuse affects us and how to respond properly to abuse disclosure. I also organized The Courage Conference to encourage survivors of abuse. I correspond frequently with victims and survivors, connecting them with the resources they need to find healing and safety.

I want you to know in your bones that you are not alone. I want you to have a clear sense of a way forward to a better life, because whether you believe it or not, you deserve to be safe and happy.

I want you to know what your options are, so you can feel a sense of control and empowerment to make your own choices. Chances are, someone else is making choices for you, whether by force, guilt, or manipulation.

I want to place the reins of your life back in your hands where they belong. In spite of what some might tell you, you are capable of making the best decisions for yourself when you have the tools, knowledge, and confidence to do so.

I want you to be able to live to your full potential as well, free of the crippling weight of abuse. I want the pain of trauma to lessen as you find support and resources. I want you to be empowered to make your own choices, to live a full and happy life.

I want you to be free.

Love and peace,
- Ashley Easter

P.S. You are stronger than you think. Many of us are out here waiting for you with arms open wide, offering love and healing.

Chapter One

Is This Abuse?

The first step in freeing myself from abuse and finding healing was allowing myself to entertain the question, "Is this abuse?" To some, this may seem like a simple question or may appear to have an obvious answer, but from the inside of an abusive relationship, nothing is simple or obvious.

Abusers have a way of getting inside your head and convincing you that you deserve the treatment you are getting, that it isn't abuse, or that it didn't actually happen at all. Abusers have a way of making the abnormal seem normal or deserved. They rationalize their behavior so much that their victims start to rationalize their behavior as well. To even entertain the thought, "Is this abuse?" or "Do I deserve to be treated this way?" is not only a big step in the right direction, but possibly a confirmation that you, in fact, are not in a safe relationship.

Many abuse survivors have what I call a *gut feeling*: this little bit of intuition or sense of nagging inside that something is not quite right. They may not have put the words "Is this abuse?" together, but they have asked questions like: *Did I deserve to be hit? ... Is it normal to feel afraid or nervous around my partner? ... Was that touch appropriate? ... Why do I feel like I'm crazy when I am around them? ... Men don't experience abuse, do they? ... Is it normal for them to monitor and check up on me so regularly? ... Would God approve of how I am being treated?*

Some experience these gut feelings at the beginning of a relationship, and others develop these feelings over time. Sometimes, internal or external voices try to explain them away or bury these questions beneath a load of excuses and explanations, but this check inside of you is a red flag that deserves to be heard and taken seriously.

As a general rule, I believe that if something feels wrong, even if you can't put your finger on it, it probably is. At the very least, it is worth asking a few more questions to make sure. You never know what pain you might save yourself from in the long run if you take the time to explore these issues now and open yourself up to the possible answers.

Defining Abuse

Abuse means to "misuse, or to treat in a harmful, injurious, or offensive way"[1] and is a broad term that encapsulates many damaging behaviors. The harm comes in several different forms, and below are definitions and examples. Keep in mind, I am not a mental health professional. This list is not exhaustive and the examples are just a few of many. If you want more counsel on your situation, I encourage you to take a look at the resources listed at the back of the book and reach out to one or more of them.

Physical Abuse

Hitting, slapping, shoving, grabbing, pinching, biting, hair pulling, physically blocking, et cetera are types of physical abuse. This kind of abuse also includes denying a partner medical care or forcing alcohol or drug use upon him or her.

Sexual Abuse

Coercing or attempting to coerce any sexual contact or behavior without enthusiastic consent. Children cannot consent; adults who are incapacitated cannot consent; the mentally or physically disabled cannot consent. Sexual abuse includes—but is certainly not limited to—marital rape, attacks on sexual parts of the body, forcing sex after physical violence has occurred, treating one in a sexually demeaning manner, non-consensually showing sexual body parts, or forcing the victim to expose his or her own.

Digital Abuse

Sexting (sending or requesting nude photos to a minor or a nonconsenting adult), child pornography, forced viewing or participation in pornography, revenge pornography, online bullying, threats, sexual harassment, or stalking.

Emotional Abuse

Undermining an individual's sense of self-worth or self-esteem. Emotional Abuse includes–but is certainly not limited to–constant criticism, diminishing one's abilities, name-calling, gas-lighting (crazy making), or damaging the victim's relationship with loved ones.

Economic Abuse

Making or attempting to make an individual financially dependent by maintaining total control over financial resources, withholding the person's access to money, or forbidding the person's participation in school or employment opportunities.

Psychological Abuse

Causing fear by intimidation; threatening physical harm to self, partner, children, family, friends, or pets; damaging of property; and forcing isolation from family, friends, school, or work.

Verbal Abuse

Vehemently expressing condemnation or disapproval, using word games, or invalidating another's point of view. Verbally abusive speech usually implies the anger of the speaker and stresses the harshness of the language.

Spiritual Abuse

Using a position of spiritual authority to manipulate, control, dominate, harass, or humiliate instead of guide and nurture. Spiritual abuse may also include misuse of religion for selfish, secular, or ideological ends.

It is important to acknowledge that other actions, not mentioned in these definitions, may also qualify as abuse.

The Ultimate Objective for Abuse: Power and Control

People who perpetrate these forms of abuse may offer various reasons for why they choose these harmful behaviors, but these often only distract from the main purpose of their abuse. For abusers, the ultimate objective is to gain power and control over their victim. Key abuse researchers believe that power and control are the underlying motivations for abusive behavior.[2]

Victims frequently believe abuse comes as a result of them angering or provoking their abusers; therefore, abusers respond to the victim's aggravation by expressing their displeasure in the form of violence (violence can be emotional or physical). Thus, victims will often see themselves as causing the anger and eliciting the abuse. Abusers then invite and even affirm that the victim's action or inaction is, in fact, the catalyst for their own violent behavior. Let me be clear: this narrative is false. Victims never cause abuse.

Unfortunately, many communities reinforce this unhealthy and inaccurate message. We see this myth perpetuated when abusive individuals are told to participate in anger management programs that only focus on addressing the symptom (anger) but not the motivation for anger. The underlying problem, however, is not that the victim induced the abuser's wrath or even that the abuser has a temper, though this may be an issue.

Rather, abusers are under the impression that they have a right to power and control over others. Any infraction of this power and control is viewed as a great offense to their perceived rightful privilege. Abusers see others, especially their victims, as subjects in their kingdom with the sole purpose of submitting to their will.

When we look at abuse from this angle, we begin to understand abuse on a deeper level. We quickly realize that it is not the victim provoking abusive responses but rather, the abuser holds a warped view of relationship dynamics. Crimes, such as sexual abuse, are not ultimately motivated out of sexual desire but a lust for power and control over a victim. Emotional abuse is not a mere miscommunication but a deliberate attempt to manipulate the victim's feelings and responses. Spiritual abuse isn't a zealous devotion to a sacred text but an exploitation of the text to control others.

Anger, sexual desire, religious devotion, or lack of communication skills may be present in the abuser, but these are only expressions of the root cause: an untamed appetite for power and control over others. The victims are not at fault for abusers' deviant outlook on relationships or the methods they use to enforce power and control. The victims are not in the wrong for defending themselves against the abusers' attempts to dominate. The victim is never responsible for correcting or trying to heal the abuser's selfish outlook.

It is important to note that society ascribes power to certain figures such as clergy, teachers, bosses, government officials, law enforcement, et cetera. With this power imbalance comes the possible danger of these figures misusing their power. For example, clergy may solicit sex from congregation members (even adults); bosses may inflict emotional abuse under the guise of company leadership; law enforcement may use unnecessary physical violence, et cetera. Abusive behaviors are still wrong, even when perpetrated by those in powerful positions, and in some cases, the very nature of their position may disallow lay people to consent to their actions, such as in the event of clergy[3] or teachers engaging in sex with adult or child parishioners or students.

Abusive Systems

Abuse is usually not an isolated incident (though it can be) but often follows patterns and occurs in cycles or phases. Below are three typical cycles or phases of abuse. If you think you may have been in an abusive relationship, and when I say relationship I mean the term broadly - romantic, familial, platonic, business, religious relationships, et cetera - I encourage you to see if any of these abusive structures fit your experience.

While these are common patterns of abuse, other patterns may exist.

The Cycle of Violence⁴

I often see The Cycle of Violence in domestic violence situations, and it frequently keeps victims on the hook in abusive relationships. This cycle gives the victim a periodic taste of goodness during intermittent bad behavior. In the end, the appearance of kindness or goodness is just a method to keep the victim prisoner to abuse and violence.

1. The Honeymoon Stage

The relationship likely started off in *The Honeymoon* or *Calm Stage*. At this juncture, the relationship is calm and often pleasant. The abuser may work hard to gain the victim's attention, showering him or her with gifts and accolades. In this phase, the victim may feel off balance and overwhelmed by affirmation. Victims are led to believe that this is how the relationship will always be and that the abuser intends to continue the grandiose treatment towards them. In essence, this is the bait used to draw in the victim. Even if there are warning signs, the mesmerizing force of this wooing behavior overpowers any red flags.

2. The Tension Building Stage

In this stage, tension begins to build. It may start small with slightly controlling behavior, jealousy, withholding, harshness, or accusations. Victims start to feel as though they are walking on eggshells, trying not to upset the abuser. This stage may be confusing to victims who just left a stage where they were praised and validated.

3. The Violence Stage

Eventually, the tension builds to a point where the abuser and victim enter *The Violence Stage* with more clear and devastating abuse. This violence is not limited to physical abuse but may be emotional, sexual, spiritual, financial, verbal, or a combination of these. Abusers strike with direct force and may seem to lose control of themselves entirely. They may literally use physical force, block the victim's exit path. They may have harsh, verbal explosions. In an emotionally violent phase, abusers may turn up the heat with their mind games and guilt trips. A spiritual abuser may enforce a "biblical punishment" such as intense indoctrination, Bible bashing, or excommunication. A financial abuser may crack down on the victim's ability to maintain a job or access to money for needed supplies. A sexual abuser may culminate *The Violent Stage* in increased sexual exploitation or more forceful sexual violation.

4. The Reconciliation Stage

After abusers have enacted a rage of violence against their victim, ensuring full power and control, the abusers may seek to reconcile with the victim. They may apologize, cry, excuse, or rationalize their behavior. They may buy the victim gifts, beg for their forgiveness, or promise to get help. If the violence was physical, they may even treat the victim's wounds and portray a loving, compassionate persona.

5. The Calm Stage

At this point, the abuser and victim may reenter *The Honeymoon* or *Calm Stage*. The abuser may continue to flatter the victim with praise and accolades, or they may simply go on with life like *The Violent Stage* never occurred, but soon *The Tension Building Stage* will begin again, and the cycle will repeat.

The Cycle of Violence may vary in length. It may extend over many years, days, or weeks and in some cases, it may happen in a matter of hours. The duration of *The Honeymoon* or *Calm Stages* may last much longer than the actual *Violence Stage*, convincing the victim that the abuser truly is getting help or that the violent times are worth enduring for the reward of the good times. In other cases, the cycle may happen so quickly or erratically that it keeps the victim off balance and unable to anticipate what is going to happen next.

Many victims are good-hearted and empathetic. The abuser may exploit this in the Cycle of Violence, convincing them that staying in the relationship is helping to heal the abuser. Other times, the force of violence is a cause of great fear, and *The Violence Stage* may intensify with each cycle, further controlling and dominating the victim with fear, guilt, or shame.

Sexual Grooming Steps[5]

Another system of abuse is called Grooming. Grooming is typically used to describe the gradual sexualization of a relationship to exploit the victim. This term has often been used to describe the way adult perpetrators court their child or teen victims, but Grooming can be observed in adult relationships as well.

1. Choosing A Victim

Predators will start by targeting an individual for the purpose of sexual exploitation. To many, it may seem that the predator's choices are random, but in reality, many predators choose their victims carefully to lessen the likelihood of being caught. Predators look for vulnerable people such as the hurting, the emotionally neglected, the sexually naive, or the isolated. It is also easier to choose victims with little oversight or interaction with family or close friends.

2. Building Rapport

Once predators have chosen a victim, they will then work to establish a relationship with a positive rapport.

They may attempt to insert themselves into the victim's life as a friend, caretaker, mentor, or teacher. In many cases, they will seek to establish trust not only with the victim, but also with those close to them, such as parents, family, and friends. Predators are sly and may take this stage carefully, slowly integrating themselves into the victim's life while simultaneously disarming the victim's support network.

3. Filling A Need

By this time, predators are keenly aware of the victim's needs and vulnerabilities. They take this opportunity to fill a void. The predator may shower a victim with time, attention, and affirmation if he or she is emotionally neglected or has low self-esteem. If the victim or their parents are financially unstable, the predator may bring the victim gifts, pay for events, clothing items, or other costly experiences. If the victim feels overlooked, the predator may pull strings to land him or her a job, business deal, or connection opportunity. Predators become increasingly necessary in their victim's life as they fulfill the victim's needs or desires.

4. Isolation

Once predators have built a level of dependence with the victim, they can begin to isolate him or her. Predators may create seemingly innocent situations where they are alone with the victim. This alone time seems reasonable to the victim given the deepening relationship, and enforces further dependence and intimate emotional connection. The victim begins to feel as though this relationship with the predator is unique and different from the other relationships, which further disconnects the victim from the rest of the world or at least creates comfort around frequent times alone.

5. Sexualizing The Relationship

The next step is adding sexual elements into the relationship. These may be subtle at first. They may occur during isolated periods or even in public. Perpetrators may start with a long gaze into the victim's eyes, a slightly longer hug, an arm around the shoulder, or a hand on the thigh. The victim becomes desensitized to these small, physical interactions. When these are enacted in public, perpetrators further desensitizes their victims as victims often feel others would say something if the interaction were inappropriate. Slowly these subtle, public touches turn into isolated situations and steadily begin to become more and more overt. A hug becomes pressing the victim's body into theirs or resting their hand on sexualized body parts. A hand on the leg may turn into touching intimate parts. Looking long into the victim's eyes may turn into a kiss. Before the victim realizes what is happening, the subtle sexual touches eventually turn into openly sexualized behavior, ultimately fulfilling whatever sexual desire the predator intended.

For young children, this process may take place in the form of a game like tickling or pretending to be a doctor, swimming in the nude, or playing to the child's natural curiosities about sexuality. Young children are particularly vulnerable because of their nativity and trust of adults in their life which makes them easy targets for predators.

6. Ensuring Power and Control

Once predators have successfully sexualized the relationship, they then seek to keep it quiet for further exploitation. They may do this by telling the victim their relationship is special and they cannot tell anyone because others would not understand. They may warn that if someone finds out, the victim will get in trouble, or the predator, whom the victim has grown to love, would be punished. Predators may resort to using threats, saying that they will hurt or kill the victim and/or loved ones if the victim tells. The predator may not even have to say anything as their religious or secular position of power over the victim may speak for itself.

Grooming is a very deceptive process and displays the forethought and deliberate intent of many predators. Predators are not always rash in their behavior and may take months or even years to groom a victim.

Stages of Indoctrination[6]

Indoctrination is typically used to maintain power and control over groups of people. It is generally seen in group abuse rather than one-on-one abuse. I see examples of Indoctrination in religious environments, cults, family sects, political movements, and even governments. Indoctrination usually takes place in a group with a centralized ideology or doctrine. Traditionally, these groups have had a centralized leader, but with the expansion of the Internet and the resulting access to information, I feel it is more accurate to say these groups are bound by similar doctrine and may be enforced by a variety of leaders. These groups may vary in size, ranging from a few people to many thousands.

1. The Recruitment Stage

The Recruitment Stage is meant to entice victims to the controlling group for the purpose of Indoctrination. Some victims are attracted by promises of happiness, hopes for change, a sense of belonging, or higher levels of spiritual enlightenment, personal power, or rewards. Other times, victims will be confronted with threats of disaster or destruction (physically, spiritually, or politically), with the controlling group presenting itself as the only way of escape or salvation. Recruitment may occur through literature, personal relationships, bait and switch marketing tactics, or mass media marketing. In extreme occasions, victims will be recruited through physical force or capture. Others may simply be born into the controlling group.

2. Isolation

In *The Isolation Stage*, the controlling group begins Indoctrination by weeding out outside influences, ensuring they can shape the victim's reality. They may start *The Isolation Stage* by claiming others outside of the group are dangerous or worldly. Some groups will present victims with perceived important tasks such as devoting considerable amounts of time to learning the group's dogma, saving the world, or defending the group against attacks. These tasks quickly take up all of the victim's opportunity for time with people outside of the group. In extreme cases, victims may be placed in solitary confinement, entirely cut off from the world through forced *Isolation*.

3. Breaking The Will

After victims are successfully isolated, a time of breaking their wills begins. The controlling group seeks to cleanse the victim's mind of independent thought when it breaks the victim's will. They may do this through subtle emotional manipulation, belittling of opposing views, using a reward and withhold system to reinforce ideas and actions they deem appropriate, or punishing those who offend their world view. If the emotional control does not work, the controlling group may enforce other forms of discipline such as substantial mental abuse, deeper *Isolation*, interrogation, deprivation, physical or sexual abuse, torture, deprivation of sleep or food, forced labor, humiliation, or threats. The goal is to bring the victim into total submission to the controlling group in thought, word, and action. There are examples of this in cult-like environments, but the idea of "breaking the will" of children can also be found in some Christian fundamentalist families.[7]

4. Indoctrination

Once victims are recruited and their will is broken, they are now ready for full-on *Indoctrination*: a reprogramming of the mind where old or conflicting information is thrown out and replaced with a flood of thoughts, beliefs, ideas, or intentions of the controlling group. Some refer to this as mind control because victims are no longer allowed to question or think for themselves. Their thoughts and actions reflect only the will of the controlling group's ideology. Victims may be forced to read and memorize dogma, sit through lectures and sermons, or have intense interrogation with the purpose of "correcting" and replacing thoughts and ideas that oppose the group.

5. Commitment/Submission

After victims are indoctrinated, the controlling group then seeks their allegiance through total submission. At this point, victims may be given a job to prove their devotion, such as recruiting others, fighting physical or ideological wars, practicing religious rites, defending the group or leaders, and in some cases, even sacrificing their lives for the group or ideology.

6. Shunning

If—at any time—victims begin to second guess, question, or defy the group and accompanying ideology, it will be seen as treason. They will be subject to *The Will Breaking* and *Indoctrinating* phases yet again. If victims reject the controlling group and can make an escape, they will be subject to *Shunning*. They will be cut off by other members of the group, and they will be shamed, guilted, and demonized to the others who stay behind. In other cases, the group will shame, guilt, harass, stalk, or even "love bomb" (an attempt to entice the victim with gifts and niceties) them instead of cutting them off. In this instance, victims will have to choose to cut ties or else be subject to continued emotional abuse. Other extreme groups will forcibly hold the victims who wish to leave or who reject *The Will Breaking* phase. They may even end a victim's life for non-compliance. If the victim escapes and can shed the group's control, the group will attempt to control others' perceptions of the victim through character assassination, rumors, and lies.

Common Symptoms of Abuse

Abuse takes a toll on the victim. Similar to an illness, abuse has many symptoms. Below are just a few typical responses our bodies and minds may experiences alongside of abusive behavior. If someone has experienced any of the types of abuse previously discussed, including any of the cycles and systems, they will likely experience several of the common symptoms that follow.

Physical Evidence

Bruising, scars, broken bones, doctor or hospital visits, or attempting to hide these things.

Fear or Anxiety

Being afraid around a particular person, having a fear of men, acting timid and careful, not wanting to go home or to a certain place, general anxiety and nervousness.

Depression

Crying, feeling down, blocking out the world, talking about or attempting suicide.

Disinterest in Something Once Loved

Not spending time alone with friends or family anymore, missing important appointments, not participating in previously enjoyed activities, not wanting to leave home.

Dissociation

When a person is unable to remove themselves physically from a threatening situation, they will often attempt to leave the situation mentally or imagine distance and safety by blocking out the abuse from their mind and thinking of other things as a coping mechanism.

Post Traumatic Stress Disorder (PTSD)

Waking and sleeping flashbacks of the event, avoidance, being easily startled, angry outbursts, feeling nervous, difficulty remembering exact details surrounding parts of the abuse, depression, negativity, guilt, and self-blame. For children, PTSD may be misdiagnosed as ADHD, and may cause regression such as bedwetting or language deterioration, or it may entail acting out the abuse in play or becoming clingy or distant.

Making Excuses

Explaining away suspicious behavior or injury, covering for other's actions, attempting to justify things out loud for their own benefit.

Weight Loss or Gain

Losing or gaining weight quickly, showing signs of illness, or seeming to "grow old" in a short amount of time.

Interventions
Police frequenting their home, victim always moving from place to place (hiding).

Overly Apologetic
Always assuming that things are their own fault, apologizing unnecessarily, frequent self-blaming.

Self-Esteem Issues
Putting one's self down or trying to elevate one's self unusually (though not in the presence of the abuser).

Change in Personality
A usually outgoing person acting shy or timid around their abuser, or an often articulate person having trouble expressing thoughts and feelings.

Developing Addictions
Turning to alcohol or substance-abuse to numb the pain.

This list is not comprehensive as there are hundreds of ways a person may respond to abuse, but this is a broad list of symptoms to help victims begin to recognize how their bodies and minds may be reacting to the abusive trauma they have experienced.

Can you identify with some of these examples of abuse? If you have, you are not alone. As you can see from these definitions and cycles, abuse has brought a lot of harm into your life. Every survivor needs a coach and help as they break free. I am here to walk with you through the tough questions and any difficulties you may encounter as you find safety and healing after abuse. Defining what has happened is a great start, but there is more healing to be found. Let's keep pressing onward—together.

Chapter Two
Why Was I Abused?

When I began to read about the different types of abuse, I started to realize more and more that the treatment I had been experiencing was wrong. It came as a shock to me when I finally was able to admit to myself that I experienced abused. I hadn't thought it was possible for me. I had never considered that I could have multiple abusive experiences. Somehow, the treatment had always felt wrong, but the abusers had assured me that these behaviors were normal. They used Scriptural justification or blamed me entirely for their abusive behavior.

As questions flooded my mind, my first thoughts swirled around the question, "How could this have happened to me?"

I grew up as a "good church girl." I went to church on Sunday morning, Sunday night, Wednesday night, and just about any other time the doors were open. I wore my skirts to the knee or below and covered any hint of cleavage, so as not to "tempt" men into lusting after me. I took messages about sexual purity to heart and worked hard to keep myself from immortality or even the appearance of it. I didn't attend wild parties or take chances with strangers. The only men I spent any time around were "good church people" too.

"Good little church girls who follow all of the 'rules' don't find themselves in abuse situations," I thought.

Except I did. And far too often, when I tell my story to others, whether they grew up in church or not, they whispers, "Yeah, me too."

According to the Abel and Harlow study 93 percent of sex offenders describe themselves as "religious"[8] and The Church Law and Tax Study found that child sexual abuse has been the number one reason churches or religious organizations have ended up in court.[9]

My abuse happened in a religious context, but maybe yours did not. Abuse does not discriminate. Abuse can happen to anyone of any color, any socioeconomic background, any religion, any sex, or any sexual orientation.

Before addressing why abuse happens, it's important to establish why abuse doesn't happen because these misperceptions are so common. Abuse isn't about you being in the wrong place at the wrong time. It's not about your background, your choices, who you are, or what you have done. In fact, abuse isn't a victim's fault at all. You do not deserve the abuse you experienced.

Abusers, and sometimes even close friends or family, may try to tell you that the abuse was your fault but this is simply not true. You are a human being deserving of love and respect. Your clothing choice was not asking for it. Your questions, disagreements, and life choices were not deserving of it. Your talking back didn't call for it. Your submission wasn't an endorsement. And your dependence on the abuser didn't give them a right to harm you.

Abuse happens because the abuser has a lust for power and control, and they choose to enforce dominance over their victim through force or manipulation.

Abuse happens because the abuser has a lack of respect for the victim's life, dignity, and free will. The full weight of responsibility for abuse always falls squarely on the shoulders of the abuser, not on the victim. Victims do not tempt, provoke, or cause the abuser to hurt them. Abusers make their own choices to abuse.

As mentioned before, the underlying motivation for abuse can always be reduced to lust for power and control. People who refrain from managing this desire act out abusively. Warped thinking and unmanaged psychological disorders commonly contribute to mismanaging the desire for power and control.

Warped thinking is present when people believe that they have a right or duty to exert power and control over another with perceived social, moral, or practical justification. Warped thinking may be present in those with impaired judgment, such as a substance abuser or an alcoholic.

The symptoms of several psychological disorders, such as Narcissistic Personality Disorder, include the need for both public affirmation and authority over others.[10] Of course, this is not to say that all people who have psychological disorders will be abusive. Many are not.

Though warped thinking and unmanaged personality disorders may (or may not) contribute to the abuser's likelihood to mismanage their desires for power and control, these factors do not excuse the abuse in any shape or form. These factors never obligate victims to stay with their abusers in the hope of helping them heal.

You are not alone either. Many victims have experienced stories similar to the one you have lived. I felt alone and isolated until I began reaching out for help and found other survivors who shared similar experiences. Later on, we will talk more about how to connect with a healing community, but for now, I just want you to hear these words.

You are not alone. It was not your fault. You are not crazy. You don't deserve to be treated that way. You are not damaged goods. You are not broken beyond repair. You are not second class. You were not born to be the object of someone else's warped desires. You are not finished. This is not the end of the line.

You are special. You have value that no one can take from you. The world needs you and your gifts. You can find healing. You can start again. You can chase your dream. There is love out here, even if you've never felt it before. Many survivors and advocates are waiting to welcome you with hope and healing.

You are not alone.

And, just in case you were wondering, just in case someone, even your own mind, is telling you that the abuse was God's will, I am here to tell you that God did not intend for you to experience this pain. In fact Jesus suffered physical, spiritual, sexual, and emotional abuse at the cross. He understands our pain. I don't have all of the answers. I'm still asking questions and searching for the right theological framework to explain how this all could have happened with an all-powerful, loving God, but here is what I do know: When I was questioning whether the abuse I suffered was God's will, and at a low point, I felt the Spirit tell me,

I don't condemn you. I get why this is hard. You've been through a lot. I just want you to know that I love you, and I'm here for you. I want to be near to your broken heart. I am compassionate to your crushed spirit. I understand that you have trust issues and questions. It's ok. Let me comfort you. I'm not like them. I won't do anything to harm you. I've got your life in my hand. Don't worry. I'm here now. Let me hold you close when you are ready.

"The LORD is close to the brokenhearted and saves those who are crushed in spirit." -Psalm 34:18 (NIV)

Chapter Three

What Should I Do Now?

Maybe you are beginning to recognize that some of the treatment you have been experiencing is not ok. Perhaps you have identified it as abuse, or maybe you prefer to think of it as unhealthy, hurtful behaviors. Either way, this can be a very overwhelming realization, and perhaps even more overwhelming is the question of, "What should I do now?"

Maybe you feel trapped in a relationship or particular environment. You want this abusive behavior to stop, but you feel like there is nothing you can do, no one you can reach out to for advice or help. It is a powerless feeling when you don't know how to improve your situation or what to do next.

I started getting flashbacks to an abusive experience. One night, I told a person close to me everything that happened, and asked them, "Does that sound normal to you?" They confirmed what my gut had been telling me all along, what happened to me was not ok. Talking with a supportive person gave me the courage to reach out to several professionals and advocates who knew how to help me and guide me through the situation. Because I reached out for help, I was able to make safe choices for myself and my future.

As a friend and as a coach, I want to show you a way to get your power back. I don't want you to feel helpless anymore. No matter what anyone tries to tell you, you are capable of making smart choices for yourself; you just need the right tools and information to help you decide how to move forward.

1. Get To A Safe Place

The first step is to get to a safe place. A safe place might be a literal, physical safe place, a mentally safe place, or both. Either way, you need space away from the abuser or group to have time to hear yourself think and consider your options. Abusers like to get into your mind and dominate your thoughts. They try to squelch free thinking and replace it with guilt, shame, fear, and confusion. They like to isolate you from outside influences, but they also like to overwhelm you with their own influence.

Maybe you can find some alone time to assess the situation and come up with a plan without the abuser interjecting their poisonous ideas. If you can safely do so, I recommend taking some time to yourself as soon as possible. In many cases, this can only happen with physical distance. If you are in a physically or sexually violent relationship/group, or the abuser has threatened to physically or sexually harm you in the past, it is imperative that you get to a physically safe place where he or she cannot hurt you.

It can be hard to leave a situation like this, whether it is because of fear, guilt, or lack of resources. Remember that, once you have distance, it will be easier for you to make informed choices regarding further contact with the dangerous group or individual. You will be able to think more freely with time and space away from the abuser(s).

Note: when an abuser or abusive group senses that you are considering leaving, they will often become enraged. This escalation can be one of the more dangerous times for a victim. Please read the next step for safety purposes.

2. Acquire Backup

If at all possible, don't take any of these measures alone. Acquire backup. I don't know what kind of situation you are in or how imminently dangerous this particular abuser or abusive system is. Because of this, I am going to suggest several options to you. Only you can know what is going to be the safest route for your particular situation. Trust your gut on this one. Despite what abusers may say, you know how to make healthy and safe choices for yourself.

In some cases, you may use only one of these options, and in other situations, you might need to use a combination or even all of these forms of backup. The important thing to remember is this: recovering from abuse is hard work. It is easier to find safety and healing when you have a support system cheering you on and caring about what happens to you. Additionally, expert support can sometimes determine life or death in a dangerous situation.

Friends and Family

Depending on the situation, the abuser may have isolated you from friends and relatives. Especially if you are in an emotionally abusive relationship, think back to friends or family who seemed skeptical of the abuser or voiced concern about the abuser to you. Maybe it was someone who asked a lot of questions about the abuser or didn't like him or her for a reason the abuser explained away. The main idea is to connect only with friends or family whom you believe will be supportive of you. You don't want to reach out to someone who has historically sided with the abuser. Listen to your gut about this too. Who is your gut telling you is safe, even if the abuser or the abusive system has tried to convince you otherwise? Seek out friends and family who are empathetic and justice-driven, if possible.

However, family, friends, and intimate partners perpetrate a large percentage of abuse.[11] I am so sorry if this is the case for you. Please know that blood relationships don't define family and that there is hope for you to find safe friends and true family in the future. If you do not feel safe asking for help from your current friends and family, there are other great options for support and comfort outside of the traditional view of family relationships.

Victim Advocates

My favorite suggestion for those in abusive relationships, or those who have experienced abuse in the past, is the support of trained abuse victim advocates. They are uniquely equipped to understand and empathize with the trauma that victims have experienced. Family and friends can be great, but they don't always know what to say. Sometimes their well-meaning words and suggestions can fall short and be unintentionally hurtful. Victim advocates are great when the trauma is still raw because they are often very careful with their words and understand better what things could be hurtful or triggering to the victim or survivor.

Advocates are also in tune with the resources available to the victim or survivor. They are often able to help the victim gain a clearer perspective on the abuse they experienced. They can then suggest relevant resources such as test kits for rape victims, free educational literature, support groups, places to stay, et cetera, or they can formulate solutions for the victim to consider such as safety plans, protection orders, alternative housing offers, or transportation.

There are multiple types or advocacy programs. Some offer support for nonemergency situations, and others can be reached through 24/7 hotlines, which are available whenever the victim is ready or needing help, even if the situation is urgent.

Many trained victim advocates are skilled at helping victims plot an escape that is safest for their situation. It is not always safe or possible for victims to leave on their own. Many times a plan needs to be put in place for leaving and finding a safe location. Advocates can assist you with this.

Advocates can also help you with making choices about contacting the police. If your situation calls for police intervention, they can assist you with how to go about it or what to say if you don't know what to do. Please take a look at the resources and advocates listed at the back of this book.

Police and Law Enforcement

If you are in a physically or sexually abusive relationship, or if you are restrained from leaving a particular place either through force, blocking, or threats, it is a good idea to contact the police right away. These situations can progressively become more dangerous or even deadly. If your life, body, or someone else's life or body is in danger, calling 911 is usually the best option. Even if the situation calms down, it is ok to call the police and have them escort you to a safer location. Calling the police directly is usually the best option for these types of situations as help can get to you much faster. Sometimes a matter of minutes could be the difference between life and death or serious injury.

Whether or not you contacted the police during the abuse, it is often a good idea to reach out to them after you get to a safe place. Advocates can help you work through your reporting options with this as well. Ask advocates about direct reporting, blind reporting, or having an advocate make the call for you to set up an appointment. Advocates have even been known to accompany victims as support when they inform the police about the abuse they experienced.

Trust your gut. When in doubt, call the police.

Legal Defenders

Depending on your situation, a legal prosecutor may be a support option for you. They can help you look at your options for both civil and criminal lawsuits, as well as protection orders, legal separations, divorce, or child custody issues. Trained victim advocates will often be able to recommend good lawyers to contact. Many times, the state automatically assigns a lawyer to the victim's case. There are also programs where victims can receive legal defense for free. I recommend enlisting an attorney who has specific experience in abuse cases as some will not understand the complexities of the issue. The first few lawyers I spoke with did not know how to support victims of abuse properly, but I was able to find some who were very helpful. Again, an advocate can be very helpful with finding a supportive lawyer.

3. Warn Others

Have you ever flown in an airplane? When the flight attendants close the doors to the plane, one of the first things they do is go over all of the safety measures in case of an emergency. They talk about how to connect your seat belt, where the exits are, and what to do if the plane is losing oxygen. The attendant will show you where an oxygen mask will fall from the ceiling and how to secure it to your face for breathing. Attendants always instruct you to fasten your own mask before helping others. If you begin helping others before you secure oxygen for yourself, not only are you more likely to pass out, but you will be less effective at helping others.

A similar dynamic happens in many cases of abuse. Often times, the abuser is hurting multiple victims. When victims are planning an escape from the abuse, it is imperative that they take care of themselves first. If other victims decide to put on their own metaphorical oxygen mask and leave the situation with you, then that is fantastic. However, staying in an abusive environment and attempting to convince others who are unwilling to go could be dangerous, as they may alert the abuser of your betrayal and you may lose precious time for escaping. After you get to safety, then you can look at your options for helping those left behind in the abusive relationship. Not only will you be stronger and in a better place to assist them, but you will often be able to bring in your backup: friends, family, advocates, police, or lawyers.

An exception to this general rule would be if you are an adult victim and you know of child victims. If at all possible, bring them with you to safety, even if they are unwilling.

Once you are safe, it is a good idea to talk to an advocate about whom you should warn regarding the abuse. Has a crime occurred or has the abuser threatened to commit a crime? Are people in danger? Are children involved? If so, it is imperative that you contact the police and/or social services.

If the abuser can harm others but the police are unable to respond in your situation, speak with your advocate and consult a lawyer who is familiar with abuse to discover the best way to warn others about the dangerous person.

No two abuse situations are exactly alike, and I don't know the details of your experience. What I do know is this: when in doubt, try to make contact with a safe person like a friend, family member, advocate, or the police. Getting an outside perspective will help you feel less alone. Speaking with a trained advocate will contribute to making you aware of your options so you can make the smartest choice for yourself. When you are isolated, the abuse situation can feel overwhelming and paralyzing, but reaching out for help from trained professionals can open your mind to options and a way forward.

You deserve to feel safe and respected. If you are ever in an abusive situation, if you have left an abusive situation, or are unsure if you experienced abuse, please contact a professional so you can take control back for your life. You can find support and safety.

Chapter Four

What Are My Rights?

To review a foundational concept, the motivation for abuse is always power and control. Abusers are obsessed with doing what it takes to maintain their own perceived rights, even at the expense of the victim's rights. Everyone has personal rights, and no one has the right to take rights from others.

Abusers are so confident about what they deserve and how the victim should accommodate them. Abusers often feel a strong sense of entitlement, and victims can become unsure about what rights they have and where the abuser is infringing upon their rights.

I want to put aside any confusion. Here are your rights as an individual:

You have the right to be RESPECTED

Whether you are a woman or a man, a child or an adult, you were made in the image of God. You have inherent worth. There is nothing you could do—and there is nothing anyone could do to you—to take away an ounce of your personal value. Because you are human, you are worthy.

Society, and sometimes even religious groups, will try to tell us that there is a hierarchy between people. Some will say that your gender, your sex, or your race determines your value. Some will say that women, because they are females, are less deserving of respect than men. They claim that women's duty is to to submit to men, or that abuse is acceptable if women do not obey a male authority. Some will say the same about different races, sexual orientations, ages, or physical abilities/disabilities. This is simply not true.

There is no hierarchy of value among humans. Each

person should be equally respected as a human being.

You have the right to THINK FOR YOURSELF

If anyone ever tries to tell you that you do not have a right to think for yourself, watch out. This is a dangerous person. Part of being human is having the right to independent thought. You have the right to question, to disagree, to ponder, to develop opinions, to research, to discover, to change your mind, to pursue knowledge, and to learn. You have the right to listen to varied viewpoints, to believe your emotional indicator, to feel your own feelings, to ponder your gut intuition, and to form your own conclusions.

You have the right to MAKE YOUR OWN CHOICES

Certainly, as an adult and in some cases as a child, you have the right to choose for yourself. It is often important to listen to the thoughts and wisdom of others, but at the end of the day, you should be able to make your own choice for yourself, as long as that choice is not encroaching on the rights of others.

It is important to differentiate between free choice and bounded choice.[12] With free choice, you can make decisions for yourself without fear of punishment, guilting, shaming, or retaliation. With free choice, you may be subject to natural consequences (good or bad) for your decision. With bounded choice, you are subjected to scare tactics, punishment, guilting, shaming, or retaliation if you choose differently than the abuser. Bounded choice is another form of control.

You have the right to choose what food goes into your body, what clothes you wear, and what medical procedures you engage in. You have the right to decide to enter or leave a relationship or organization, to remove yourself from a place or situation, and to make choices about your education.

You have the right to
SET BOUNDARIES

Boundaries are choices that you make for yourself regarding relationships and interactions with other people. Boundaries are like dividers that say, "Do not cross this line." Boundaries allow you to maintain relationships in ways that are safe and comfortable for you.

Here are a few examples of boundaries: We can be friends, but I will not share certain details about my life with you ... You can hold my hand, but I am not ready or willing to let you kiss me ... We can have a conversation, but only if you are respectful ... You make me feel unsafe, do not contact me ... I don't want to have this conversation right now, give me space.

Boundaries help to keep you emotionally and physically safe. You do not need to apologize for having boundaries, and others should respect your chosen boundaries. It is also ok to move your boundaries forward or backward at any time. For instance, when you first go on a date, your boundary may be "You are not allowed to kiss me;" as the relationship progresses, you may decide to move your boundary line to "I am now comfortable with you kissing me."

Just because you have moved a boundary in one direction doesn't mean you can't move it back. Let's say your spouse would like to have sex, but you are not in the mood. You can move your boundary again to say, "No thank you; I do not want to have sex right now." Boundaries can even change in the moment. At first you decide you want to have sex, so you both take your clothes off, but then for some reason you change your mind. It is ok to move the boundary again, "I changed my mind, and I am not ready to have sex right now" or, "I know we had this type of sexual interaction in the past, but I don't want to do that right now. I would prefer this instead."

You have a right to set boundaries, to say yes or no. Others have the responsibility to respect your boundaries, and you must respect theirs. Sometimes people call these boundaries *consent.*

This is how I understand consent:[13] The presence of an enthusiastic "yes" (verbal or non-verbal) void of manipulation, power plays, threats, or head games; not just the absence of a "no." Additionally, children cannot consent to sexual activities with adults or older children.

Consent isn't just about sex; it is about setting boundaries for all areas of life.

You have the right to YOUR BODY

Keeping in line with our conversation about boundaries, you have the right to make choices for your body. You have the right to decide how you dress it, what you feed it, what medical interventions affect it, and who does or does not touch it.

You have the right to BE SAFE

You have a right to safety for your body, mind, and soul. Anyone who wishes to hurt you physically, mentally or spiritually, or to put you in a place where you do not want to be, is encroaching on your rights to safety from danger.

You have the right to HEAL

You have a right to choose methods of healing that are right for you. You should be able to recover at your own pace. You should be able to process and heal in your own unique way. No one should be able to dictate how long this journey takes you, what feelings you are allowed to feel, or what methods of healing are most beneficial to you. This is your journey, and no one else can map out your healing path for you.

*Exception: Others may need to enforce programs or medical interventions for healing if your life or others' lives are in danger.

You have the right to
DISCONNECT FROM ABUSE

If you are in an abusive relationship or an abusive group, you have the right to leave or put space between yourself and whoever is harming you. Some people may pressure you to stay in abusive relationships or organizations. For the sake of the marriage … For the sake of the ministry … Because you owe it to them ... Because they depend on you … Because you are a Christian … Because you should be more forgiving … Because you are family … Because you should try harder to fix things … Because you made a promise … Because you… If someone is abusing you, no matter who they are, you have a right to leave because they are violating your rights to be treated with respect and to set boundaries that you feel are in your best interests.

How do you feel after reading these rights? It might be hard to believe right now, but these rights belong to you. I hope that as healing comes, you feel more and more empowered to live in the freedom these rights bring and choose people in your life who honor your rights as a worthy person.

Chapter Five

What Should I Expect From Others?

Reaching out for help and support during or after abuse is a brave and vulnerable step. For this reason, it is an honor to be entrusted with another person's story. This privilege comes with responsibility. It is my wish for you that those with whom you choose to share your story will realize this and honor the confidence you have placed in them.

The first reaction to abuse disclosure can make a huge difference in someone's life. It can determine whether or not they feel excessive amounts of shame, and whether they get the professional help they need.

In this chapter, I would like to lay out the proper responses you should receive when disclosing abuse, and how to address improper responses if they arise.

Inappropriate Responses to Abuse Disclosures

Victim Blaming

Blaming is a response that places full or partial responsibility on the person who was or is being abused, instead of putting the full measure of culpability on the abuser (where it belongs). It is important to remember that there is nothing a person could ever do (or not do) that could make them deserving of or responsible for the abusive actions of another.

Victim Shaming

Shaming attempts to humiliate or dismiss the victim by drawing attention to the victim's imperfections, whether real or perceived, and away from the abuser. Shaming simultaneously applies the letter of the law to the victim and disproportionate grace to the abuser.

Victim Silencing

Silencing is an attempt to quiet the victim's voice in a selfish effort to save the abuser and others from embarrassment or consequences.

Examples of blaming, shaming, and silencing:

- If it was so bad, why didn't you just leave or say something sooner?
- You are a bitter, crazy, delusional, emotional, imaginative, or forgetful woman.
- You are a man, and *real* men do not experience abuse.
- Your job, clothing, life choices, belief system, relationship choices, or sexual orientation indicates that you were asking for the abuse.
- You enjoyed or benefited from parts of the treatment. Therefore, it wasn't abuse.
- The person you are accusing isn't capable of that; they are a godly and respectable person who has helped others.
- You must have misunderstood.

- If you speak out, you will destroy a ministry, business, organization, reputation, family, or faith.
- "X" Bible verse says it wasn't abuse; you should just submit and obey.
- "X" Bible verse says that talking openly about abuse is gossip or slander.
- If you don't heal or handle the abuse our way, you are wrong.
- You will not be believed, so you should not speak out.
- Your story seems unlikely or confusing; therefore, you are lying.
- You are the only one speaking out, so you must be lying.
- You have changed, added, or remembered details since you first came forward, so you must be lying.
- You didn't realize it was wrong at the time, so you can't change your mind now.
- You did not respond perfectly before, during, or after the abuse, so you don't have a right to speak out against the other person.
- You should just forgive and forget.

Appropriate Responses to Abuse Disclosures

- Report to law enforcement or social services when necessary.
- Contact a licensed professional who regularly assists abuse victims.
- Offer to help the victim connect with community resources, counseling, and medical services.
- Offer empathy and compassion.
- Respond in gentleness and patience.
- Offer a quick ear and a slow voice. Listen well and speak slowly.
- Respect the victim's wishes and choices.
- Support the victim's personal healing process.
- Offer encouragement if the victim speaks out or chooses to heal quietly.
- Defend quickly against others who seek to blame, shame, or silence the victim.
- Give space when needed.
- Be willing to learn about abuse.
- Follow-up after the initial disclosure.
- Remove the abuser from places of power and

authority when possible.
- Take away opportunities for the abuser to intimidate or re-offend.
- Above all else, take the victim's story seriously.

Proper Responses From Family and Friends

Dianne was molested by a missionary colleague of her parents. When she told them about the sexual abuse perpetrated against her, they believed her and reported the abuse to their mission leaders. Dianne's perpetrator confessed and seemed remorseful, so the mission board refused to remove him lest it "destroy" his ministry. The mission board also used the argument that "all of us sin," so Dianne and her parents should forgive and move on. Dianne's parents refused to return to the mission field with that organization, knowing that Dianne would be forced to be around him again if they returned. Their actions on her behalf - putting her before their ministry - was a key component in her healing journey.

When telling a friend or family member about the abuse you experienced, the appropriate response to your story should be empathy and care. It is typical for friends and family members to feel shocked or anger towards the abuser when they hear how you have been treated. Friends and family are not always equipped to know what to do next, but they should respond with empathy and a willingness to support you through your healing journey. Ideally, they should recommend that you speak with a professional (an advocate, the police, or a counselor) and offer to go with you. However, not all friends and family will realize this. Even if they are not sure how to respond, they should not be resistant to you seeking professional support or addressing the abuse.

Improper Responses From Family and Friends

Michelle (name changed to protect her identity) attended a Bible study with her mother. While the women met in the living room for the study, nine-year-old Michelle was left alone to occupy herself in another part of the home. The Bible study hostess' husband tragically molested Michelle several times. Michelle finally found the courage to tell her mother.

Unfortunately, her mother's response was, "Let's not tell Dad." When Michelle brought it up again sometime later, her mother said, "Well, maybe that didn't really happen." After that, however, she did keep Michelle with her during the Bible study. Michelle was later violently raped as an older teen. She never told anyone, thinking to herself, "What's the use? It won't make any difference anyway." This abuse as well as the negligent response from her mother had a tremendous effect on Michelle's life, including numerous hospitalizations for depression.

Many times, family and friends are uneducated about the topic of abuse, so it is understandable, though difficult, for them to have questions. These questions, however, should not come from a place of doubting your story or blaming you for the abuse you experienced. Family and friends should not ignore, refuse to believe, or refuse to help you. They should not continue a close relationship with the person who abused you. Family and friends should not discourage you from seeking professional help, from sharing your story in ways you deem fit, or from setting boundaries that are healing for you as an individual. Family and friends should not pressure you to reconcile with your abuser or attend gatherings where the abuser is present.

Proper Responses From Churches

For many abuse victims and survivors, churches and other places of worship are an integral part of their life. The abuse may or may not have occurred in the church, but survivors typically reach out to clergy for advice and support. A church that responds properly will take time to hear the victim's story; they will offer empathy; and they will direct the victim to professionals such as advocates, professional counselors, and police. If the abuse was perpetrated by a church member or leader, the pastor to whom the abuse is disclosed should submit to the advice and direction of law enforcement and contact professional victim advocates such as GRACE (Godly Response to Abuse in the Christian Environment) who are skilled at handling these situations. Churches will remove the perpetrator/alleged perpetrator from any places of leadership in the church. They will forbid the individual from attending church functions where the victim or other vulnerable people will be present. They will warn others (such as parents) if the abuser/ alleged abuser had or has access to children while the offense is being sorted out by professionals. The church should seek to support and protect the victim instead of sheltering the abuser.

Improper Responses From Churches

In a high profile abuse case involving a medical doctor affiliated with the ABWE mission board and a young missionary girl, the organization had the child sign a "confession" alleging her involvement in "her affair" with the doctor. She was only 13-years-old when the abuse occurred. This was not an "affair" but a case of sexual assault. Children cannot consent to sexual activity with adults. ABWE treated the victim as if she were complicit and as if she willfully engaged in the crime. They pressured her, under stressful circumstances, to sign a statement that was styled as a "confession" when she had nothing to confess. There is no evidence of any ABWE personnel attempting to assure the victim that she was not at fault for her abuse.[14]

Unfortunately, not all churches and Christian organizations respond correctly to abuse disclosures. Some church leaders will disbelieve, shame, blame, or attempt to silence the victim. Some churches will seek to guard their own reputation and the reputation of the abuser instead of properly supporting the victim. Churches have been known to try to handle the abuse in-house instead of reporting abuse to the proper authorities, including the police. They may wrongly try to counsel the victim or rehabilitate the abuser instead of connecting them to professional counselors. Some churches seek to brush abuse under the rug or send the abuser away quietly instead of taking the issue seriously and involving outside professionals like police and trained advocates. None of these responses are ok, and none of them reflect the heart of Jesus.

Proper Responses From Advocates

Advocates have been an integral part of my healing. Good advocates will listen non-judgmentally and offer relevant support and direction. They will have a good understanding of what your options are in your particular situation, or they will know who to contact for better care.

Advocates will be able to guide you in the right direction, toward safety and healing from a place of educated understanding. They will know about your options regarding police reportings, counseling services, or legal defenses, and advocates can connect you with them. At the end of this book, I will be listing several quality abuse victim advocate groups whom I believe will give you excellent guidance and service recommendations.

Improper Responses From Advocates

Though I have not encountered these issues, I would deem an advocate inept if they didn't listen carefully and empathetically, or if they minimized, shamed, or blamed the abuse victim. If this is the case, or if the advocate is unable to recommend services and professionals relevant to your situation, or if they are unsure of how to guide you out of an abusive environment, I recommend insisting to be connected with another advocate.

Proper Responses From Law Enforcement

Police officers should quickly respond to emergency situations and positively respond when a victim brings abuse to their attention. When I reported an instance of abuse to the police, I had an encouraging inter-action. I decided I wanted to give them my story in written form before our meeting, and they were accepting of this because it was most comfortable for me. They were willing to have the session with my victim advocate and a friend present for support, and the officers even allowed me to choose a location where I felt comfortable. They asked me questions about my story but did so in a compassionate way and assured me the abuse was not my fault. They looked over my case, got back to me in a timely fashion, and gave me precise information about what could and could not be done based on the details of my event. They were respectful and kind during the entire interaction and told me I was right to report the abuse to them.

Improper Responses From Law Enforcement

Many officers are kind, ethical, and efficient, but this is what it would look like if they were not. An inadequate response from the police would be a tardy response to an emergency situation. It would be wrong for an officer not to take your story seriously or not to interact with you in a respectful, understanding way. Blaming and shaming would also be a wrong response from the police. It would not be ideal for an officer to be long in responding or unclear in describing to you your rights and options based on the situation. If you should run into an officer who responds poorly, ask your advocate for advice; they may be able to direct you to a more competent, respectful responder.

When you tell your story, you deserve to receive a proper response. If this is not the case, I beg you not to give up. Keep asking until you find someone whom you can trust, someone who offers you both the empathy and the support you deserve. Please take a look at the recommendations at the end of this book.

Chapter Six

How Can I Move Forward Towards Healing?

After you have removed yourself from an abusive relationship or an abusive environment, you might think that the pain is finished. However, for many survivors, reaching safety is only the beginning of the healing process.

Survivors may develop a variety of feelings in abuse's aftermath. A common diagnosis for survivors is Post

Traumatic Stress Disorder (PTSD). This is the same response many military veterans experience when coming out of combative situations. If you think about it, the comparison makes a lot of sense. Experiencing abuse can feel like living in a physical or mental war zone.

PTSD may include, but is not limited to, waking and sleeping flashbacks of the event (also called triggers), avoidance, being easily startled, angry outbursts, feeling nervous or anxious, depression and negativity, guilt and self-blame, and difficulty expressing exact details surrounding parts of the abuse.[15]

I want to stop for a second to make a few remarks about the last symptom in the list—difficulty expressing exact details surrounding parts of the abuse. This is a very common side effect that may bring confusion to both survivors and those listening to their story. There is a reason why this happens. When our bodies experience trauma[16] (including abuse trauma), we could have several different involuntary responses: fight, flight, or, the less commonly known, freeze. For some, the reaction to trauma is to attempt to fight off the predator. For others, it is to try to flee the situation. These responses are reactions from different parts of our brain. Our response to abuse is often something we cannot control. It just happens automatically based on how our brain decides to react. In other cases, our brain tries to signal us to both fight and flee at the same time. Because we can't do both at once and two different parts of our brain are responding at the same time, the differing signals cause our body to freeze involuntarily. This is why many victims don't leave the trauma situation. Their brains are trying to protect them, but they are overloaded, so the victim just freezes during the event. In addition to the body freezing, the brain is functioning abnormally, which may cause the victim to have blocked or disorganized memories of the traumatic experience. This can be very frustrating, but it is our brain's defense against attacks. The brain is trying to protect the victim from danger, so it is working overtime. Suppressed or disorganized memories may occur as a safeguard to keep the victim from being completely overwhelmed by the situation. Just know that this response is normal and even expected.

In addition to PTSD, survivors may experience grief and a sense of loss. It can feel like a death—perhaps a death to a relationship, a dream, childhood, marriage, a church relationship, or trust and security.

Grieving abuse may feel similar to grieving the death of a loved one. An abuse survivor may go through the stages of grief including shock, denial, pain, guilt, anger, depression, adjustment, reconstructing life, and then acceptance and hope.[17]

If you have experienced abuse, you are likely still feeling the pain of the event. My heart goes out to you. I've been there, and I am still on a healing journey. I want to tell you; it gets better. Trying to forget that the abuse happened and burying your emotions may seem like the best option at the moment, but the pain will always be under the surface, ready to pop up later, unless you take steps towards healing.

Each person has their own North Star. Each person has a different healing journey, different paths, different speeds, different tools, and different techniques. If you want to start your healing journey but are not sure how to begin, I'd like to present you with a variety of tools and options to help you get on the right path to a peace-filled life.

Tools for Healing

Seek Professional Counseling

Counseling by a licensed professional is, in my opinion, the best first step in the healing journey. I look at it this way: if a person experienced a physical injury or was suffering from an infection, the best first step would be to visit a medical doctor. In this metaphor, abuse is like the injury, the damaged emotional and mental health after abuse is like the infection, and the physician is the licensed counselor. Just as it would stunt or prevent the physical healing of an injury to go without proper diagnosis and treatment, so can avoidance of this step prevent or hinder healing from abuse.

A licensed counselor can give a diagnosis to help survivors correctly understand their experiences. In the first chapter, I gave some broad definitions of abuse, and a survivor may be able to identify some of the types of abuse they have experienced. A professional can and should give a full diagnosis. You could think of it this way: Googling medical symptoms can give people an idea of what medical issues they are having, but it is still best to see a doctor who has training in that area. An untrained person may have missed something or misdiagnosed the problem entirely. Not only can a doctor identify the medical issue, they can also come up with a proper treatment plan and give access to a variety of tools that an untrained person would not have. In counseling, a professional can both diagnose the issue and assist you with healing. Professional counselors can help you develop useful coping strategies that are not dangerous in the long term. Counselors have a variety of treatment types that they can offer, and they may even suggest other specialists who can help you through new technology, such as EMDR therapy.

I want to give a word of caution. Just because people say they are counselors doesn't mean they are qualified to address abuse. Some churches will have pastoral counseling or biblical counseling (also known as Nouthetic counseling), but these individuals are not sufficiently trained to address abuse. Even if they mean well, you wouldn't want a person treating you for a medical issue unless they had a degree to prove their scientific training as well as experience working with your medical problem. The same goes for mental health counseling. Not only can their treatment be less effective, it can even be dangerous to allow an unlicensed counselor, without specific training in abuse and trauma, to attempt to help you heal from abuse and trauma.

A good counselor can put you on a path towards healing, one that is much faster than if you tried to do it alone or with the help of an untrained individual. For me, counseling has been a positive experience. I had to try more than one counselor before I found one that was right for me, but when I did, it was dramatically helpful in my healing.

I recommend interviewing counselors over the phone before meeting in person. I like to make sure our personalities click and that they have the proper credentials to help with my issues. I look for someone who has experience assisting with abuse and trauma, PTSD, depression, anxiety and has an egalitarian view when it comes to marriage relationships. I recommend asking an advocate for recommended professional counselors in your area. If money is an issue, let them know. There may be income based payment plans or free options in your area.

Always remember it is important that you feel safe with the counselor you choose. If you don't feel safe, or if you are not clicking with the individual, it is always ok to leave and try someone else. Additionally, it is possible to outgrow a counselor as you progress, and you may need to switch to someone with more experience who can attend to your specific needs.

Research the Effects of Trauma

A good counselor will educate you on the specifics of the trauma you are experiencing. You can also ask for book recommendations, or you can search for articles online. I write at www.ashleyeaster.com, and many of my posts are about abuse and healing from it. Researching the topic for yourself can be an empowering option. Learning for yourself why your body is responding the way it is can give you a sense of control and clarity when your life is feeling out of control. Researching for yourself can give language to some of the feelings you may have trouble expressing. It can also give you new topics to cover in your counseling sessions.

Tell Your Story

For some survivors, telling their story is both healing and empowering. Abusers try to define the narrative of our life and steal our story. Telling our story either out loud or in writing allows us to take back the narrative. Some prefer to tell their story to a few people who are close to them. Others prefer to speak about it more loudly and publicly. Either is a legitimate way to tell your story. If you choose to go the public route, either through writing or speaking, I recommend talking with a lawyer to make sure you know what the impact of your words could be. I recommend consulting a lawyer who is skilled in abuse situations because others may brush off the importance of the issue. Remember, your story is your own. You have a right to tell it how and to whom you wish.

Connect with Other Survivors

Some of the most healing experiences for me have been when I have met with fellow survivors. I have been to several conferences addressing abuse, including The Courage Conference which I founded, and walking into a room with other abuse survivors was a breath of fresh air. We all knew we had something in common, and we could bond over our shared experiences. There is nothing like hearing other survivors share their story and having that "me too" moment. Connecting with others eases the loneliness that survivors often struggle with and validates our feelings.

You can connect with other survivors through events like The Courage Conference (www.TheCourageConference.com). Other ways include survivor groups that domestic violence centers often host, online private forums, closed Facebook groups, group therapy, or you could start your own group, though I recommend having a trained advocate on hand in case things get emotional and people are in need of assistance. Take a look at the resources suggested in this book, and consider reaching out to an organization or two for information on support groups if this interests you.

Explore Different Types of Churches or Spiritual Resources

If your abuse intersected with faith, that can be particularly painful. I know for me, certain translations of the Bible or even paper Bibles altogether are triggering to me. The old church I attended was not a safe place for me, and even the denomination I was affiliated with had painful ways of presenting the Bible. Despite these circumstances, I have found healing while still keeping my faith. I attend a different church and denomination that feels safer to me. I like to read from a different Bible version, and usually I do this on my smartphone instead of out of a paper book. I have allowed myself to explore the various communities and perspectives within Christianity, and this has been very healing. I discovered that the Scripture passages used against me in spiritual abuse have completely different meanings than I had been led to believe.

Sometimes I have been so disappointed with the way

the church responded to my abuse that I just needed a break. That is ok too. God understands and doesn't judge you for it. Jesus himself experienced physical, emotional, spiritual, and sexual abuse at the cross, so I believe he is very understanding and compassionate towards your pain.

Create

I have seen survivors create pure beauty after abuse— from artwork, to poetry, to music, to dance, to books, to businesses, to nonprofit organizations. While creativity can never excuse or justify the painful experiences, survivors often create beauty where there once was none, and it is stunning.

Personally, I have taken to writing about healing on a blog. I've created poetry, sung songs, preached messages, and founded The Courage Conference. You could even say this book you are reading is one of my redemptive creations.

Here is the important part: not only am I creating for others, but I am creating for myself. Each new creation bears a piece of my soul and is a healing salve to my wounds. Creating helps us heal; it tells our story; it combats evil with love and beauty. Creating declares that you will overcome the darkness by making light, and that you will form healing connections in direct defiance to the isolation which abuse administers. Creating is the opposite of destruction, and it is a terrific blow to the destroying nature of abuse.

Reach Out and Help Others

When you are farther down on your healing journey, reaching out to help others can be both rewarding and restorative. I cannot tell you how many inspiring, redemptive stories I have heard from survivors of abuse. I think it is in our bones. When we begin to heal, we wish to bring others along with us. We look abuse in the eye and say, "Not only did you fail to destroy me, but now I will rescue others from your clutches." For many of us, reaching out to help others is how we win.

The best victim advocates I know are also survivors. I have met a survivor who experienced abuse during a medical visit and now works in a medical facility, making sure it doesn't happen to others. I have seen a survivor who was told she could not preach, but now is asked to preach healing messages across the country. I have seen survivors create global anti-trafficking initiatives, start women's empowerment groups, and teach children about consent. The list goes on and on.

Maybe it would be healing for you to consider finding your own special way to reach out and support others, for their healing and your own.

Be Gentle with Yourself

Sometimes we are so concerned about others that we neglect to care for ourselves. Sometimes abuse has dragged our self-esteem through the mud, and we aren't even sure if we like ourselves. It can be hard to extend love and compassion inward. It can be hard to be gentle with ourselves when others have been anything but gentle.

Here is a little tip I use. I try to look at myself as a friend. I ask myself questions like: What would YOU like to do? ... What do YOU think about this? ... How do YOU feel? ... Does this feel safe for YOU? ... Are YOU hungry or thirsty? ... Do YOU need to rest?

I ask myself these gentle questions and listen for the answers. It is not selfish to take care of yourself. You deserve care just as much as everyone else. Sometimes, when others abuse or neglect us, we internalize that behavior and inflict abuse upon ourselves. This is understandable, but it isn't fair. You and your body deserve to be treated with kindness and respect, especially from yourself. So be gentle with YOU.

DEAR FRIEND,

Thank you for you allowing me into your heart for a few chapters of this book and for a few chapters of your life. I realize what a privilege this is and I don't take it lightly. I hope that you found this little book to be helpful and clarifying. I hope that you have new knowledge and a few more tools to help you make safe and respectful choices for yourself. I hope this book starts a new chapter in your life, a chapter full of safety, hope, and healing.

I want to close by giving you some words of encouragement:

You are NOT alone.

You are valuable.

You are loved and worthy of love.

No one can take your value from you.
You deserve to find support.
You deserve to be heard and believed.
You deserve to find healing, and I sincerely hope
you will.

Love and peace,
-Ashley Easter

Resource List

AshleyEaster.com

Read about my journey and other articles on healing from abuse and discovering gender equality.

The Courage Conference

The Courage Conference is a non-denominational event that will offer a judgment-free place for survivors of abuse (and those who love them) to gather and hear inspiring stories from other survivors about moving forward in boldness and healing. The event will also educate pastors and church leaders on the topic of abuse and introduce them to safe practices and resources for their faith community. TheCourageConference.com

GRACE (Godly Response to Abuse in the Christian Environment)

Private investigations of sexual allegations, presentations, resources, church safety certification program, information on child sexual abuse and perpetrators. www.netgrace.org

Christians For Biblical Equality International

An organization equipping churches and individuals with tools and resources on gender equality and ending patriarchal based abuse. CBE also provides a list of egalitarian counselors in the U.S. www.cbeinternational.org

MK Safety Net (Missionary Kid Safety Net)

Help for missionary kids abused on the mission field. www.mksafetynet.org

Together We Heal

Support for any who suffer from the trauma of childhood sexual abuse. It exists to provide guidance and counseling to those in need.
www.together-we-heal.org

Voices of Consent

Bringing awareness to sexual assault and providing care packages for survivors. www.voicesofconsent.org

Healing Broken Men

Support and recovery groups for male survivors. www.healingbrokenmen.com

National Sexual Violence Resource Center

Resources and education on sexual abuse.
www.nsvrc.org

Domestic Shelters

Search engine for locating abuse prevention and response centers with trained advocates. www.domesticshelters.org

Hotlines

National Suicide Prevention Hotline (USA)
    call: 1-800-273-8255
    chat: www.suicidepreventionlifeline.org

The National Domestic Violence Hotline (USA)
    call: 1-800-787-3224
    chat: www.thehotline.org

RAINN National Sexual Assault Hotline
    call: 1-800-656-4673
    chat: www.rainn.org

The Crisis Text Line
    text: "START" to 741-741

Endnotes

1 http://www.dictionary.com/browse/abuse.

2 http://csnjh.org/domestic/; http://www.
virginia.edu/sexualviolence/relationshipviolence/
dynamics.html; http://www.intervalhouse.ca/news/
general-news/is-domestic-violence-about-power-
and-control; https://www.gov.mb.ca/justice/victims/
domestic/pubs/cycleofviolence.pdf; http://www.
theduluthmodel.org/training/wheels.html.

3 http://www.baylor.edu/clergysexualmisconduct/
index.php?id=67406.

4 https://www.domesticshelters.org/domestic-
violence-articles-information/faq/a-deadly-cycle#.
WKIJXhIrLR0.

5 http://www.naasca.org/2011-Articles/010911-6StagesOfGrooming.htm.

6 http://www.icsahome.com/articles/arousal-capacity-baron-csj-18.

7 http://religiouschildmaltreatment.com/.

8 http://religionnews.com/2014/01/09/startling-statistics/.

9 http://www.churchlawandtax.com/web/2016/august/top-5-reasons-religious-organizations-went-to-court-in-2015.html?utm_content=buffer394a4&utm_medium=social&utm_source=twitter.com&utm_campaign=buffer.

10 https://psychcentral.com/disorders/narcissistic-personality-disorder-symptoms/.

11 http://www.ncadv.org/learn-more/
statistics; https://www.rainn.org/statistics/
perpetrators-sexual-violence.

12 http://quiveringdaughters.com/
exploring-bounded-choice/.

13 https://www.rainn.org/articles/what-is-consent.

14 ABWE and Donn Ketcham Investigations Final
Report by Pii.

15 http://www.mayoclinic.org/diseases-conditions/
post-traumatic-stress-disorder/basics/definition/
CON-20022540.

16 https://purposefullyscarred.com/2015/10/15/
trauma-and-the-brain-understanding-why-a-
victims-story-might-change/.

17 https://www.adams.edu/administration/hr/img/7-
stages-of-grief.pdf.

DISCERN / DEFEND / DELIVER

www.TheCourageConference.com

Ashley Easter

ashleyeaster.com

Be part of a community of world-changers, truth seekers, love wranglers, and liberators.

Made in the USA
Coppell, TX
08 January 2021